WE HAVE MADE MUSIC

WE
HAVE
MADE
MUSIC

by

Theodore M. Finney

UNIVERSITY OF PITTSBURGH PRESS

Library of Congress Catalog Card Number: 55-12433

CONTENTS

PREFACE

IF these little essays need any introduction they need two: one for the small host of young people who have been members of the Heinz Chapel Choir at the University of Pittsburgh; another for the "stranger" who may happen to come across them. The two prefaces will have one thing in common: they must both speak of education.

For those who have been a part of the choir, I need only to reiterate that here are some of my attempts to "review" for you a part of your education. The word "education" has come to have many meanings in our modern world, but it still retains the original sense of being a process of drawing forth qualities latent in the individual who is being educated. For you I have cared mostly that we find something of your very best; I need now only to tell you that you had it all the time!

*   *   *   *

For others, I should like to suggest that perhaps these essays, which originated as talks at choir banquets or Sunday services at camp, have general implications beyond the particular situation from which they arose.

Liberal education seems to have a tendency to lose its way among the analogies which control much of our thinking about it. Insect societies have held a strange fascination for man, since perhaps even before the injunction, "Go to the ant," and it is possible that we have learned either too much or not enough from

7

some of our analogies. The worker ant probably does her job *instinctively,* and nature has provided her with no further abilities, nor need for them. She is "integrated" by virtue of the loss of general over-all competence which results from her specialization. Specialization has to be *learned* by human workers. But beyond that, human beings seem to have a need for much more: for all sorts of devices for developing and communicating the ideas and feelings by which they wish to live. Perhaps a liberal education lies in the area beyond that which the worker ant has mastered by instinct.

One should, I suppose, admit the possibility that those of us who think we think are wrong. Maybe all there is to culture is to build more elaborate nests, continuing to divide ourselves on the basis of how elaborate they can get. But I think not; there is still the dream, there is still Santayana talking to Socrates about the "love and need of a special perfection in each creature's heart." And perhaps drawing out this "love and need" has something to do with a liberal education.

*   *   *   *

Probably the following pages do not contain enough quotation marks. Any personal attitude toward living must be in debt to countless minds whose earthly immortality is in our care. The writers of the Bible—it is still the Bible when it is a metrical version from the ancient Scotch Psalter—and William Shakespeare and Robert Burns and Heinrich Heine are above any danger from my need to lean on them. I have felt free to quote without permission from one of the many memorable sermons of William Robertson Farmer, and from letters from my friends. I am conscious that such letters are the property of their writers, but by allowing them unembarrassed anonymity I am willing to risk the theft. They are teachers and by now must be reconciled to such pilfering.

I am grateful to publishers of copyrighted material for permissions granted invariably "with pleasure": Charles Scribner's Sons of New York, for lines from *Dialogues in Limbo* by George Santayana; Longmans, Green & Co., Inc. of New York, for extracts from *Human Destiny* by Lecomte du Noüy; Constable and Company Limited, London, England, for a short paragraph from *The Architecture of Humanism* by Geoffrey Scott.

Hundreds of other obligations growing out of the silences, the tones of voice, and the facial expressions of my young friends will have to be understood by them. But I must write the names of Mrs. Agnes Lynch Starrett and Miss Barbara E. Millen of the University of Pittsburgh Press in acknowledgment of their help without which this could not have become a little book. And I could not close the account on this list of my debts without thanking "Jimmy," Miss Marion L. Blasing, for her patient expertness in translating my handwriting.

Theodore M. Finney

"*Man, as the savage first conceived him, man, as the mind of science still affirms, is not the centre of the world he lives in, but merely one of her myriad products, more conscious than the rest, and more perplexed. A stranger on the indifferent earth, he adapts himself slowly and painfully to inhuman nature, and at moments, not without peril, compels inhuman nature to his need. A spectacle surrounds him— sometimes splendid, often morose, uncouth and formidable. He may cower before it like the savage, study it impartially for what it is, like the man of science; it remains, in the end, as in the beginning, something alien, and inhuman, often destructive of his hopes. But a third way is open. He may construct, within the world as it is, a pattern of the world as he would have it. This is the way of humanism, in philosophy, in life, and in the arts.*"

—GEOFFREY SCOTT, The Architecture of Humanism

I

We Have Made Music

SINCE the first week of January of 1939 I have been spending what would probably average, for nine months of each year, at least six hours a week of my time standing in front of you—the Heinz Chapel Choir. Most of that time we are at work, rehearsing or singing for audiences; and when we are working I seldom have much difficulty conveying to you, in one way or another, the information that is immediately necessary to what we are doing.

On one or two occasions almost every year, though (the Sunday service at camp, the annual choir banquet), a combination of circumstances brings me in front of you when we are not working. When that happens, two kinds of ideas chase each other around in the back of my mind. One of them has to do with my amazement that you ask me when you don't have to. I should think you would get enough of me in the way of our work. I wouldn't "flunk" you—fortunately we don't worry about grades in the choir—if you let me sit back in the corner these few times that are really yours, and just watch the fun. I wouldn't flunk you, but if I am to be absolutely honest with you and with myself I must admit that I might, with this group, feel a little lonesome off in the corner.

The other idea is not really an idea at all, because I never seem to succeed in getting it to say itself completely and to my own satisfaction. It must be really an extraverbal idea, an idea of the sort that many of us poor stuttering humans struggle to find expression for but cannot, an idea that is not really expressible with words at all, an idea of the kind for which perhaps poetry and music were invented, an idea that for most of us ends with trembling cheek muscles and misty eyes.

So I keep studying, oftener than you might suspect: "How can I tell these young people how really important it is, this work that we do together and this time that we spend together?"

I wouldn't want you to think that I place too much importance on *my* finding an answer to that question. Sometimes I get discouraged enough to wonder if it is important. Most of the time though, I am not discouraged, but even then the question which involves my being able to tell you something that *I* know, is partly, I suppose, just a college professor's habitual desire to hear his own face rattle. Because you who are now in the choir, and the hundreds who have been in the choir before you, have the idea too; you know what I should like to be able to say. But you must admit that you can't get it said either.

I am going to try, though, again, for all of us.

We sing together; we make music together; our whole story, if we could endow a few trite words with a new, fresh, luminous meaning, might be said in these four:

"We have made music"

We practice four times a week, late afternoons when most of us are at the tired end of a busy day, in an unfinished, too-warm room, with not even a piano in it, and we have a marvelous time, so marvelous that the building is full of our singing from the elevator shafts as we ride down past thirty floors when we have finished.

We have made music

We are Christian and Jew, Protestant and Catholic; we are English, or Greek, or German, or Italian, or French, or anything else that happens. We are brilliant and average, homely or not quite so homely, second or thirteenth generation American; we have money or we don't have, we are Fraternity or Independent. We are prospective engineers, or dentists, or schoolteachers, or nurses, or scholars, or businessmen and women; we are engaged to be married or still free, we are tall or short, dark or light. These do not matter: color of skin, political party, social and national and religious and cultural backgrounds—none of these things matter in the least.

We have made music

We love each other—more or less. We are friends—we really care about each other. We celebrate each other's triumphs; we are hurt by each other's failures—and sorrows. I, for instance, will never forget the looks on the faces of the choir members lined up in a hospital waiting room once when Mom needed some transfusions. Neither can any of us who were there ever forget the last half of a concert we had to continue when the intermission brought the news to one soprano that her sweetheart had just been killed in an airplane accident. We all know what Sandy really means when she screws up her face and says: "I loves you madly."

We have made music

We seem to be a busy center for the activities of the little bare boy with the bow and arrow. A boy cracks a girl over the bridge of the nose with a badminton racquet at camp and now they are four. Pop warns a sweet little sophomore that Tony is a big bad wolf—and within six weeks he is the tamest dog you ever saw, and, moreover, we can't go near the part of the state where they live without coming to eat, and to admire the two sweet little towheads in the bedroom. So cupid shoots his arrows, sometimes leaves them and sometimes pulls them out (leaving wounds which seem fatal but which usually heal)—the soprano whose sweetheart fell out of the sky will marry a choir alumnus this spring—and we go on.

We have made music

We take a very real pride in our immediate work, our singing.

Because of our pride, we learn from what we do. We have to learn notes and words, and to sing those notes and words in a way that will make music, and we discover that we cannot bluff without getting caught. Our product will not be what we want if we are dishonest in our preparation. In just "getting by," the music itself convicts us of dishonesty. Other people should, I suppose, learn that too. Musicians—even such musicians as we—cannot avoid learning it.

We have made music

When we are ready to do our very best, we sometimes do even better than that. Here again, perhaps, we learn from our work itself. Twice a week we bow our heads for a moment as we wait in the basement of the Chapel, while the minister asks us to consider that what we are about to do is done for something greater than ourselves. It is possible that many of us take very little notice of that moment; it is possible that some of us are not even consciously aware that we are at times—all of us together —moved beyond our own capacities, inspired to be greater than we really are. But I am sure from my own experience with you, that when we offer our very honest best to God and His Congregation we often are helped to do better than *our* best.

We have made music

We have a training camp in the fall, with days of hard work and fun and getting acquainted. And on the Sunday morning of camp we come together for our own Service. We sing, and hear our "sub" choir sing, and hear some one of ourselves talk. We come out into the Sunday sunshine with an experience that we dare not talk about but which will, I think, for some of us remain forever poignant.

We have made music

We sing in the Heinz Memorial Chapel. It is a monument in stone and wood and glass from people who felt, I feel certain, the need to express a deep gratitude for a family tradition which transmitted the sure knowledge that the human spirit is a small

14

and insignificant thing without God. The Chapel should say just that to everyone who enters its gates. It will stand there, we hope, for thousands of years. Much of the time it stands without a voice. We, my friends, make it a living memorial to the highest aspirations of a great family, of a great University, of our own souls! When we are there, when we begin the Processional down the long center aisle, when we sing our anthem, when we respond to the prayer, when we end the Recessional with a hushed amen in the narthex, we have made the Chapel and what it represents come to life.

We have made music

And so I—or any of you—could go on, trying to give expression to what we feel about what we do together. And it could always return, like a litany, to the refrain:

We have made music.

II

Through a Glass Darkly

I HAVE called this little talk "Through a Glass, Darkly." That is not its title. But I chose it to start, in your memory, the tremendous passage from which it is taken, because in that chapter from one of Paul's letters to the Corinthians *is* the title.

Some of you have gotten it.

A former choir president wrote this in a letter to us recently:

"Occasionally I am given to reflection, and since it's been three months since the last choir was at your farm, I've thought a little about what you said to the seniors that day. You said that we were sad to be leaving, but that you were primarily sorry because we would so soon forget the choir.

"In a way I think you were right, but for one point (which may or may not be encouraging). We will forget a lot of things: the music, the things we did, even most of the people in time. This is only natural and not a sad thing. Yet another aspect is natural, too, and it is the most important, something which we cannot forget. This is an indefinable feeling that develops. It is above camaraderie or companionship. It is influenced, I think, by the environment of music. It is a type of love; perhaps it is the sense of love. Those of us who felt it will not forget it, even though the choir may fade and only be recalled with a smile or little laugh when, years from now, we pass the Chapel, hear a choir song, or see an old member. This is so."

With that, I shall try to read what I have read once or twice before.

Every year, on one Sunday in September, I am called upon to make what the Order of Service calls an "Address" to the members of a new choir. You—this new choir—are just beginning a year of work. It may turn out to be a year to remember with pride or just another year, depending on how we work together and upon how we feel toward each other and toward what we are doing. This is what I think about when it again becomes apparent that I have to talk to you on this Sunday morning. What I should like to be able to tell you is something so important to me that I can never avoid the sense of inadequacy which one always feels before important things.

The old members of the choir, and the choir alumni who are here with us today, have learned what I should like to tell you. It would be difficult for them to put into words: they would be self-conscious, as am I, but their knowledge would show in their eyes.

The choir of the Heinz Memorial Chapel of the University of Pittsburgh exists to sing in that Chapel. Our work is to the end that the worship of God may have dignity and beauty and meaning. We practice our art for the service of God. Our rewards, quite various, and at times seemingly unrelated to our chief work, really have that function at their foundation. The music we make, when we make it as we should, has important meaning only as it relates to that fundamental function.

The musician understands that the quality of a fundamental tone owes much to the resonance of its overtones. The tone will not exist without its fundamental, but once given a fundamental, quality increases—becomes rich and vivid—with the addition of overtones. This must be true also of our condition. We have our fundamental function, to lead in the worship of God, but that fundamental accumulates, *actually produces,* a series of resonant overtones which builds up a sense of tremendously rich meaning for many of us.

It is that kind of meaning—a kind of meaning really involved in our music—about which I should like to talk and before which I feel a profound sense of inadequacy.

Like most any other schoolteacher, however, I shall overlook my inadequacy and talk anyway. I shall try to tell you a little about the meanings, the overtone meanings, which have come to sound for me in just one piece of music. I might talk about this music in an altogether different way. I must, as we rehearse it, approach it from another viewpoint, but just now I am speaking not as a music teacher but as the recipient, together with you, of a vital experience. These meanings, then, are really the overtones of my experience with this piece as we have used it in our work together.

It is a simple, lovely old tune, and its words are a quaint metrical version of the Twenty-third Psalm. We sing it not oftener than once or twice a year for the people who attend our Chapel services, and to most of them it must be just another anthem. To the casual listener it could hardly be anything else. He might catch a glimpse of the feeling you young people express when you are singing not with your voices alone but also with your hearts, but he would have to live with that song as we have to know the tremendous resonance of its overtones.

That resonance grows constantly. We sang one summer in the amphitheater at Chautauqua. We were all just a little nervous about our appearance there, so for the Sunday morning service we chose to sing the anthem we all loved so well. It would be greeting a strange audience and a new acoustical situation through an old friend with whom we could be comfortable. We sang it, and very near the beginning we began to feel at home. Here, too, the Lord was our Shepherd; here, too, were green pastures and quiet waters!

Some of us knew the man who preached that day. Until recently he had been pastor of one of our own University churches. He knew us, and when he began to talk we knew even more surely what our song had done, for he spoke of us as "his favorite choir singing his favorite anthem." That afternoon we sang a concert in the same place, but, because we had sung it in the morning, we omitted Brother James' Air. We missed it, so the next afternoon when we sang again we started our concert with it. The program was informal: I announced what we were going to sing as we went along, and tried to get the members of the audience to feel as happy listening to us as we felt singing for them. While I was acknowledging their at first only polite applause, it suddenly occurred to me that it was too bad that the audience could not have the chance to begin to love our song as we did. By the time I could get to the microphone I knew what we were going to do. I told them that good music always sounds better the second time. It did, too, partly because we made it better. I didn't need to conduct the second time: I felt new overtones as I looked into the faces of the choir and saw them love their song into the hearts of the audience.

Brother James' tune and the great Psalm made the afternoon for us, as they had made the previous morning. But these overtones are just an echo of the meanings that years of singing the piece have given it.

I have made a beginning in describing where those meanings come from; now, when I try to turn back to some of them they make a procession which seems to have no beginning.

Ah! here it is:

One alumna of the choir doesn't like that song. When members of former choirs gather to see each other, and to sing together again, she frowns when we sing Brother James' Air. Her frown does not disturb me; we sang this song for the first time during the spring of her senior year. She has had no chance to live with it. Its resonance was just beginning.

Our first singings of it must have been perfunctory. But it attracted us enough so that the next year someone in the choir asked: "Pop, when are we going to sing Brother James' Air?" We sang it again, and it got into our concert program.

I used to object to the choir singing concert music informally when we were traveling. But after a train ride back from a concert I had a letter from a lady—a stranger to all of us—who was returning on the same train from a funeral. She told me how the spontaneous singing of those young people, especially of our version of the Twenty-third Psalm, had lifted her spirit, had started her out of the darkness of her sorrow. I read them the letter. I could hardly, any longer, resist too much their desire to sing when they felt like it. Brother James' Air was beginning to acquire its richness for all of us.

The late spring of 1942 was not a pleasant time. The music we made together seemed more and more important. Oftener and oftener at rehearsals we sang Brother James' Air, not with any self-consciousness—because what we did then is apparent only in retrospect—but because it was our song: it somehow seemed to hold us together against the dispersal which we knew was inevitable.

We had a choir throughout the war. What it undoubtedly lacked in tenors and basses we must have made up in the tenaciousness with which we clung to our work and to each other. We had a song ready for the victory long before we could use it. But we had not prepared an anthem to mourn the death of the only President most of the choir members could remember. The morning after the announcement of his death the Chancellor's secretary told me that there would be a memorial service at noon in the Chapel. By ten o'clock all the choir members had inquired, either in person or by telephone, about what was wanted from them. I told them to be ready for the noon service: we would know what to do when the time came. The Chaplain, hardly expecting a choir on such short notice, had planned a service so simple that the choir would not be needed, but the looks on their faces told him that they must be given their part. What would they sing? For the President whose loss they all felt that day with inexpressible poignancy, they would sing Brother James' Air. For themselves, for the students and faculty who crowded the Chapel and the yard around it, they would sing:

> The Lord's my Shepherd, I'll not want,
>   He makes me down to lie
> In pastures green, He leadeth me
>   The quiet waters by.
>
> My soul He doth restore again
>   And me to walk doth make
> Within the Paths of Blessedness,
>   E'en for His own Name's sake.
>
> Yea though I pass through shadowed vale,
>   Yet will I fear no ill;
> For Thou art with me and Thy Rod
>   And Staff me comfort still.
>
> My table Thou has furnished
>   In presence of my foes;
> My head with oil Thou dost anoint,
>   And my cup overflows.
>
> Goodness and mercy all my days
>   Will surely follow me;
> And in my Father's heart alway
>   My dwelling place shall be.

That April noon we heard our Chaplain say: "He was our President, and he is dead. He was in this terrible war our Commander in Chief, and he is dead. And we know why he is dead. We know that he fell in battle, giving without reserve the last full measure of devotion . . . . 'Moses my servant is dead. Now therefore arise and go over this Jordan, thou and all this people with thee, unto the land which I swore unto thy fathers to give them. As I was with Moses so I will be with thee. Only be strong and of good courage. Have not I commanded thee?' And now today, as we mourn the death of the man who led us thus far on our way, we are to remind ourselves that the land of Promise is still just ahead, that the longing hearts of men still strain toward it, that above all it is still the will of God that we should come into it at last and dwell there. Moses dies but Joshua takes over, and the great adventure goes on." The congregation sang the great St. Ann tune "O God, Our Help in Ages Past," and we sang "And in my Father's heart alway my dwelling place shall be."

Overtones!

This recounting could go on for a long time. Perhaps I have told enough to make my point.

This summer we counted our copies of Brother James' Air to replace the ones that have been pasted into Memory Books. We had to have enough for the new members who make this next choir. I shall teach you—perhaps already have taught most of you —the notes, and I shall show you with my hands and face how I want you to make them into music. But I can only begin to tell you the meanings it has for me. In time it will become part of your lives as it has become part of mine; your meanings for it— and I am sure for much other music too—will be as poignant as mine; we will have been together for a time "in pastures green."

III

An Elephant
And a Mouse or Two

O NE of my friends recently attempted to console me about getting old. He tried to tell me that life might be better after a certain age, which would seem very old to you, than before. The letter fell in with a kind of stocktaking I was giving myself, and it used one phrase which gives me my title and text for today. My friend was telling me what most American men have to learn, that although when they are born there is a possibility that they can get to be President, there is every probability that they won't and that somewhere along the line, if they want to achieve even a little serenity, they had better lower their sights to a target within range of their particular brand of ammunition. What he said was, in part, this; here is my text: *"I know damned well I'm not going to wash an elephant, so I'm going to wash a mouse or two to my own sweet taste, and let it go at that."*

I don't need to talk very long about the elephant. Elephants get awfully dirty about once in a generation in our country; washing one is too big a job for one man, and likely to turn out to be dirty politics. It's the mouse or two in which I am interested this morning: a mouse or two, to my own sweet taste!

A long time ago a Teacher "went up into a mountain" to converse with people who must have had at least one thing in common with me: they had given up washing elephants. They were the meek and the mournful and the merciful, who hunger after righteousness, who are persecuted for righteousness sake, who are poor in spirit and pure in heart, who are peacemakers and reviled. All those descriptions were opprobrious: those people just wanted to wash a mouse or two, to their own sweet taste. The Teacher taught them some hard lessons, and probably the climax was this: "Be ye therefore perfect, even as your Father which is in heaven is perfect."

Now it may seem to you to be pretty farfetched to suggest a similarity between what a hard-boiled journalist wrote to his friend and what the Teacher said up there in the hills. But to me at least the advice to "wash a mouse or two" suggests a continued search for perfection, and "to my own sweet taste" could be interpreted to mean that my own taste, to be sweet, must be referred to the perfection of "your Father which is in heaven."

Some of you must by now be thinking to yourselves: "What in the world is he driving at?" I am driving at what I have tried to tell you and your predecessors a good many times before. It has to do with what we understand only haltingly. Our friends—even our very dearest friends whose affection we most desire—often fail completely to understand it, and when we try to tell them they are inclined to think that we are conceited, neurotic, and even perhaps blasphemous.

We function together in a learning and teaching situation. We work at learning music, but we all know that what we learn is something more than ordinarily is meant by music. So if you are asking what in the world I am driving at, I must answer just now by asking you to consider with me what in the world is that "something more than music" that we are learning.

Is it perhaps out of this world, not really in the world at all?

Is there, in the making of music, an intimation of perfection?

The search for perfection, the need to "wash a mouse or two to my own sweet taste" begins with an apparently insurmountable difficulty. The Teacher on the mountain who summarized one of His greatest utterances with "Be ye therefore perfect," went from there straight out of this world: perfection is an attribute of God. But this difficulty is insurmountable only in the sense that it is impossible to imagine the complete achievement of perfection. To arrive at the *end* of the search is given to no man. Whatever our talent, creed, or color, the search itself can hardly be avoided. It *must* be undertaken: whether he wishes it to be so or not, a man's life is that search; every judgment we make of ourselves and of our fellows, all our and their doings, is conditioned by how we are making that search. *We must all try to wash something*.

It seems evident to me that although much of what that Teacher was saying from the high place must have sounded as visionary, as unpalatable, even as unacceptable, to many of his listeners as it may to many of us; yet He was on pretty solid ground when He said "Be ye perfect," for no matter how impossible of attainment perfection might be, He was telling His listeners to be what every last one of them, in the good and true and proud moments of his life, had been wanting and trying to be. The hopefulness of good men must grow out of their ability to continue the search for perfection; the hope that we all have for our world and for the lives we must live in that world springs from our hearts' necessity to approach some kind of perfection. When the search stops, when it is overpowered and given up, *then* there is tragedy. But even a little success in the search, even a momentary experience of fragmentary perfection, is enough to fire the heart, to tell the spirit that life can go on toward the shining adventure.

The moments which make human lives hopeful are those which point toward perfection, which tempt us to believe that after all our search will not be futile. The high moments, when things "march," when they are "in tune"; the "lift," the "kick" even; these we all know and treasure. They drive us on our quest. We wash a mouse. The elephant is too big for us, but by heaven we can wash a mouse or two.

Not long ago a book called *Human Destiny* attracted a good deal of attention, a book written by the French scientist-philosopher

Lecomte du Noüy. I would not, of course, recommend reading a book to college students, because most of you already have read a book, but reading and trying to understand this book might make you feel more at home in the world you are inheriting, especially if you could disagree with some of it. Du Noüy describes in detail how the biological history of mankind, commonly called evolution, has been a search for perfection. In summary he says: "Everything has taken place as if ever since the birth of the original cell, man has been *willed;* not as a superior animal capable of speaking and of using his hands, but as the support of the brain, the organ of conscience, of intelligence, the seat of human dignity, and the tool of further evolution. Man, with his present brain, does not represent the end of evolution, but only an intermediary stage between the past, heavily weighed down with memories of the beast, and the future, rich in higher promise. . . . All the ancestors of man were but irresponsible actors playing an imposed part in a play which they did not understand, or try to understand. Man continues to play his part, *but wants to comprehend the play*. He becomes capable of perfecting himself . . ." Man's future evolution, as at least one important scientist defines it, might have been deduced from the Sermon on the Mount, "Be ye"—*become* ye—"therefore perfect."

The whole destiny of man, then, is perfection. Intimations of perfection, wherever they may be found, if they help to direct us in our quest, are fundamentally the most important things in the world. The need for human perfection is so basic and its attainment so far in the distant future of man's destiny that he has had to invent ways to achieve it in areas which do not encompass the whole of his needs but which, nevertheless, serve to provide the intimations which make his goal seem eventually attainable. Some would say that we turn instinctively to one or another of these areas of experience for a feeling of perfection; others might say that they have been provided as part of the divine will which the great Teacher was expressing. In any case, the areas correspond to the needs of many of our human senses, and they are able to provide us with sensations which may, if we know what is taking place, give us a sustaining hint of our destiny, a sense of the meaning that resides in the command, "Be ye, therefore, perfect."

All this may sound—I hope it does sound—as if I were talking about something of really tremendous importance. That mankind may continue—that even a *few* men may continue—to strive toward a destiny of perfection in a world of almost unbelievable chaos in order to become "even as your Father which is in heaven," must be important. That men can, through a kind of mechanism which they now possess, achieve certain kinds of perfection, and thus catch a glimpse of that goal, must make that mechanism extraordinarily important.

The desire to set up standards of perfection, together with sets of rules—often seemingly quite arbitrary—is universal. Styles, codes, moral principles, philosophies, manifestos, and the like are usually attempts to provide such standards and rules. I might cite one or two examples that I have run across in my own studies.

For centuries many men felt that perfection was inherent in certain numbers. Churchmen, for instance, ascribed a very special sense of perfection to the number three, because it represented the Trinity. When medieval church musicians began to compose music in which they needed time measurements, they used only triple divisions for several centuries because it never occurred to them that music for the church could be anything but perfect. When they finally adventured into duple divisions, they called them imperfect. Some of our notational signs still indicate that concept of perfection and imperfection.

Another kind of perfection was felt to reside in certain geometrical figures, particularly the circle and the equilateral pentagon. The sign which makes a quarter note perfect—equal, that is, to three instead of two eighth notes—is really a very small circle; the "prick of perfection," the medieval penman called it.

Another device for attaining perfection was the golden division. It was a measurement by which any given line was divided so that its small part had the same relation to its large part as the large part had to the whole line: *a* is to *b* as *b* is to *ab*. The golden division was applied in designing letters, buildings, figures in perspective in paintings, even the shape of musical instruments. The modern violin probably owes its shape not to the application of scientific acoustical principles but to the use, by Stradivarius and his predecessors, of such sure and safe sources of perfection as the circle and the golden division. Who can say that the use of such seemingly arbitrary guides to perfection has not at times succeeded? The search was there!

I have been talking just now about the evidence of the universal necessity to search for perfection. The mechanisms by which we make our search are important. I want to bring the subject a little closer to us, and I am now ready to mention another of these mechanisms. It will turn out to be a subject with which I appear oftener than I do in this present function and to which I may perhaps bring a semblance of authority. I am, then, ready to name the mechanism: music.

Music—the sort of music we are making together—is a means by which we may understand a kind of perfection. We will have —have had—high moments together during which the sounds of our voices and the expressions on our faces are evidence enough that we are knowing how one kind of perfection feels. Out of that sense of perfection comes to me, and I am sure to you, too, the ability, at least momentarily, to achieve some of the meekness and mercy and love which the great Teacher said were parts of being perfect—which we know are the hard parts. The perfection we may achieve in our making music is not easy. It *should not* be easy because it is too important. It requires a steadfastness of aim, an effort of understanding, that will carry us over failures and discouragements; it requires some special qualities of heart and mind and sensitivity and even voice, but when it is rightly understood, it is important. You can prove to yourself that the achievement of perfection is rewarding beyond all expectation: beyond all expectation, that is, unless you understand that perfection wherever it is found, in no matter what small quantities, is a hint of *ultimate* perfection.

St. Augustine, in a book which is not read very often any more even in theological seminaries, said fifteen hundred years ago that music, above all other human activities, *is the truth brought down from heaven*. It must be honestly and humbly made, but given that integrity it is not prayer but answer, and cannot be frustrated by any mere human failure to understand. It is a glimpse of perfection.

Many of you know what I mean. You may know, too, that in making music in a Chapel which is another kind of perfection, it is possible to transmit your experience to others whose need for a constant renewal of faith in the search is as great as yours.

Do you suppose it is possible that we might be learning *these* things, too, as we sing together? Perhaps the earlier question should have been: "What *out* of the world are you getting at?" Because if what we do together can give us these insights it really does keep open the door of another world.

During the time I have spent turning over and writing down what I have been saying to you I have had one important reservation clamoring for admission to my thinking. I have kept it out until now, knowing all the time that it must finally appear.

It began with my saying to myself: "This is an extraordinary subject for a gray-haired man to be presenting to these young people. They are the perfectionists, not you. They want to wash elephants, not mice. You ought to be old enough to know better. You know that perfectionism is a pretty faulty, even a dangerous, and often a cruel philosophy." I could not, then, in any kind of honesty, dismiss such a reservation. I cannot even trust my humble mouse to take care of it.

Perfectionism, which is often an attribute of youth, is not quite the same as becoming perfect in either the sense of the Sermon on the Mount or of the scientist. It has about it a certain arrogance which is in keeping with neither. Intimations of the ultimate greatness of perfection must often be separated—sorted—from events and experiences and persons not always—not even often— perfect in themselves. This is also a part of human destiny. You may come to love the experience or the person more for their failure completely to achieve what the race will accomplish only after millenia of travail, because that failure really represents the shining adventure of the search.

May the hours you spend together singing be your part in what the psalmist meant when he said: "O sing unto the Lord, all the earth. Sing unto the Lord, bless His name; show forth His salvation *from day to day*." May they give you, as they have given me, not only a sense of the real meaning of perfection but the even greater knowledge that here, too, in this activity, we may move a little closer to the great destiny of mankind. We may, if you will allow me to return to my title, "wash a mouse or two."

IV

Shall Brothers Be

ONE of the parts of our work together is to learn words. Words which have some kind of musical quality or surroundings seem to be easier to remember than the ordinary earth-bound kind. Combinations of words that seem to sing have been sticking in my mind ever since I began hearing them from my mother. So when it becomes evident that I am to talk to you again on this Sunday morning, the process of finding a kind of text-title for what I should like to say brings back two lines, and underlines three words, of verses which my mother loved, and loved to repeat. It was Robert Burns, at the end of one of his last poems, saying

> That man to man, the warld o'er,
> Shall brothers be for a' that.

There is the title I couldn't seem to avoid: "Shall Brothers Be."

My *subject,* which may turn out to have some connection with my title, also grows out of our work together, but from an aspect more fundamental than the mere learning of words. It is a relationship with some symptoms from which I get considerable amusement. Perhaps the most striking one is the fact that only the unusually reticent or dignified new choir members continue to address me as "Dr. Finney" for very long after our year's work has begun. This process, which seems to be a kind of extralegal "adoption," has such by-products as my having to submit to the attempts of thirty-three young ladies trying to straighten my black tie as we wait to begin our banquet—when I know all the time that a bow tie wouldn't stay straight on me if two angels stood by and held the ends of it all evening. What I am trying to say is that a kind of family relationship begins right here. You have felt it beginning. And a family, even the size of this, implies a kind of brotherhood.

I am on dangerous ground when I begin to draw conclusions from this phenomenon, and I should be much less than honest if I did not approach what I want to say with caution. Connecting music and brotherhood can be made to sound too easy: let us all use or like music—put music in our daily diet—and we will soon arrive at brotherhood.

I am unavoidably reminded of Lorenzo's comment to Jessica in the first scene of Act V of the *Merchant of Venice:*

> The man that hath no music in himself,
> Nor is not mov'd with concord of sweet sounds
> Is fit for treasons, stratagems, and spoils;
> The motions of his spirit are dull as night,
> And his affections dark as Erebus:
> Let no such man be trusted.

This passage is not, certainly, the most quoted of Shakespeare's lines on music, possibly because it might be a little dangerous to tell a man who does not respond to music that he "is fit for treasons," that he is not to be trusted. I quote it here because it, like my subject, makes the whole matter sound too easy. You probably would expect a musician to say, either in so many words or by implication, that the way to avoid being fit for treasons is to have music in one's soul. Take a good dose of music, and your affections, the motions of your spirit, will be bright; be moved by a concord of sweet sounds and you will be a trustworthy, straightforward citizen, a brother to all mankind. This is a comforting thought. But we don't know how it works, and if we stop to think we know that sometimes it most obviously does not work at all. It adds to our admiration for George Washington to know that he had some sensitiveness to music. Carlo Gesualdo murdered his elder brother to become Prince of Venosa, Henry VIII removed his wives by what was, I suppose, a legalization of Carlo's methods, and Frederick the Great started Prussia on its "glorious" history over the dead bodies of the victims of his long wars. These men were all fairly well-known composers. They had music in their souls. And wasn't one Adolph Schickelgruber, who was often—it has been reported—"mov'd with concord of sweet sounds," fit for much worse than treasons, stratagems, and spoils.

Shakespeare's statement is, of course, negative. But even to take it at its face value is to give music more credit as a symptom than it deserves. I have never known a more gentle, honest, kindly man than my paternal grandfather, yet if he had music in his soul it most certainly was not evident when he tried to sing the hymns in church: his small grandson cringed every time the old gentleman's voice got out past his white beard.

To turn Shakespeare's words around, to suggest that music is a cure for the faults the poet lists, is perhaps hardly fair to Shakespeare; it is even less fair to those at whom the quotation is directed. Men and women are likely to be good or bad quite apart from any relation to or interest in music they may have. Until we can allay the suspicion that music may be as useful to the *badness* of some people as it is to the goodness of others, we might do well to keep fairly quiet about the whole matter. Could it be that music was for Hitler a means of throttling his remorse, his conscience, which, had it not been so lulled out of existence, might have stood in the way of the holocaust?

The truth is that music can be used and liked while it is being abused. Its highest purposes, like the high purposes of religion, can be and too often are desecrated by its votaries, violated by those who claim to love and serve it. We may at times be enthusiastic over the possibility that music might remake the world, but it is hardly in keeping with our experience to be too sure. We might well tell ourselves what Hamlet told Horatio:

> There are more things in heaven and earth, Horatio,
> Than are dreamt of in your philosophy.

Hamlet had just seen a ghost!
I, too, have been seeing ghosts!

Our civilization, our present Western world, inherits the great Hebrew-Christian tradition. Many of us have been told that the greatest contribution of the culture which originated that tradition was the conception of monotheism. What seems to me to be more important, even than that, was the gradually acquired certainty that the possession of the human *spirit,* by all the children of the one God, must be the basis for an order that respects, cultivates, and honors the dignity and integrity of *every* human being. That, for me, is the heart of our tradition: the dignity and integrity of the human spirit.

The human spirit has been building itself monuments for thousands of years. You can see some of them around you wherever human beings have lived for long. You can find them in libraries, museums, concert halls. But can you find very many of them in the hearts of men?

I have been seeing ghosts, I said a moment ago.

A quarter of a century ago I sat one day in the little garden back of the north transept of St. Paul's Cathedral in London. The building, you will remember, was begun after the great fire of 1666, and because its foundations went into wet earth, Christopher Wren had depended on the moisture in the ground to support the weight of the dome he was going to build. I had found the dome filled with scaffolding, and had been told by one of the Cathedral staff that it was too bad that my generation could not see that dome. Building the London Tubes had drained the ground: the piers supporting the dome were sinking and liquid concrete was being forced under the foundations to support them.

I sat in the garden pondering that man's words and tone of voice: a young American—we tear our buildings down and replace them in a hurry here—a young American was getting a lesson in the relation between time and the human spirit. My generation, no, but there will be many more; there are many under the stones in the crypt!

Last year I sat again on the same bench in the same garden. I had just seen the inside of the dome. But now the transept was shrouded; its stones lying around my feet. And back of me, and in front, from Cheapside clear down to the river, was devastation. This time not the foundations of the cathedral dome, but of the human spirit, of civilization itself, had collapsed. All the monuments, all the books, all the museums, all the music, all, even, of what saintly men call the "witness" of the great church itself— all had failed to halt the tempests of men's anger.

Was this the measure of my own little time: the dome repaired but the world almost destroyed? Hardly conscious that my shoes were grinding the gravel of the path under the bench, I watched the shadows shroud the dome until the rough boardings around the broken transept were brighter almost than the London sky. Then I saw the numbers painted on the stones in the garden. I heard the echo of the caretaker's voice: "this generation." The stones would be returned to their places in the ruined vaults, but not for me. This had been my generation; I would not return again. At our beginnings we had pumped concrete under rotten foundations but somehow that had not been enough. Everywhere was the evidence of our failure.

These crushing ghosts waiting for me in this quiet garden were hardly what I had come to see. But I gathered up what small momentum I could find and went on across the narrow sea and the ancient Rhine into the land of Handel and Bach and Beethoven and Mendelssohn and all the others. I had lived there, too, that quarter-century ago, very happily, learning music and some of the other things that a young man learns in a strange country. But this time it was impossible to stay—not even a minute beyond the time it took for what I had come to do.

They were digging ghosts out of the rubble. They *are* digging the black ghosts of the human spirit out of the ashes. The broken skeletons of brotherhood lie buried there among the twisted remains of a world that once had been pleasant. The people who had lived there had thought and talked much about the spirit, but they had called it not the *human* spirit but the *German* spirit, *der deutsche Geist,* forgetting, I am afraid, that in their language, even more than in ours, the same word means also "ghost"!

I wandered through the broken streets of Munich, hunting an eighteenth-century book that I needed, a book written by a cousin of Johann Sebastian Bach. I had been here, too, in that other world of my youth. But now the museums were gone, and jerry-built shacks lined the once noble streets. The skeleton of the solid old cathedral was still there, though, back of the City Hall, but no longer crowded by the busy streets of a happy city. Beyond it, fenced off, was a quiet desert of broken bricks, almost an open field where the bombers had dropped their retaliations to the denials of human brotherhood.

As I walked toward the ancient landmark—Orlando Lasso had been music director there in the sixteenth century—the lines of an old doggerel tried to get themselves remembered. I had driven my wife almost to distraction trying to memorize them from a picture post card that time before, and her laughter at my fake histrionics came back with the lines:

> So lang der alte Peter
> Am Petersbergl steht.

There were a lot more lines beginning with "as long as"; they wouldn't return. But this was enough: "As long as the old St. Peter's tower stands there on its hill." And I could remember the last two lines:

So lange stirbt die Gemütlichkeit
Vom Münchener noch net aus

"just that long the friendly spirit of the people of Munich will not die out."

I couldn't find the old St. Peter's Church; the prophecy had been fulfilled: the spirit, too, was gone. Well, of course: but the bombers hadn't done it all. Couldn't one too easily remember the beer-hall *putsch,* the murders in the streets, the shrill screams of the leader coming over the transatlantic radio answered by the mesmerized chanting of the crowd, Dachau nearby? No, once again, my memory had recalled a flood of ghosts. In this city where *Tristan* and *Meistersinger* were heard for the first time, the evidence of the failure of the human spirit was again almost overwhelming.

As I picked my way along toward the twin towers of the Cathedral, the "Mother of God," I found my inside ear hearing the thunderous monotony of one of the marvels of the timid little Viennese schoolmaster, first the music and then the words. I didn't remember then that the poet, Heine, was a Jew, and Schubert an Austrian. I guess it didn't matter; for this piece they were brothers.

> Du stolzes Herz, du hast es ja gewollt,
> Du wolltest glücklich sein, unendlich glücklich,
>   oder unendlich elend,
>   und jetzo bist du elend.
> Ich unglückselger Atlas,
> Die ganze Welt der Schmerzen musz ich tragen.

"You proud heart, you asked for this: you would be lucky, eternally fortunate, or endlessly wretched, and now you are wretched. I, miserable Atlas, must bear the whole world of sorrows."

I was dogged by ghosts! I have been seeing them ever since.

37

I couldn't stay. I found my book, and some others that I needed, and then I came home.

As I sat sleepless among strangers, pulled through the black night almost a day's ocean voyage every hour, I wondered about what *I* have done. I have made a little music—not much—but mostly I have tried to help others make and know music. It has been fun—I was hardly prepared for this crushing feeling of defeat—it has seemed as it has gone along like a not unworthy expenditure of a life. Has my experience putting music and people together taught me anything hopeful? Is there *any* hint that might exorcise these ghosts? The old platitudes won't do: their failure is too obvious. Even Shakespeare, at the end, used Ariel's music to lure Caliban into a frightful quagmire. It will not do, piously to go on soothing savage beasts! This time, this moonless night high over the Atlantic, let's try to be honest.

Music: brotherhood: the human spirit.

We *must* somehow be brothers if we want our world to survive. We repeat an ancient phrase about loving our neighbors as we love ourselves, and have forgotten what it means. When will it occur to us to remember the dignity and integrity of the human spirit? Not only our neighbor's, our brother's, but our *own*. Most of us don't know how to love ourselves. We chip off and erode our own dignity and integrity. We cheat, we make promises without really committing ourselves to what we have promised, we throw away our time, we accept half jobs from ourselves. Who, with no genuine respect for his own spirit, can honor that of his brother?

But wait a minute! Is it possible, if we know what we are about, that music might show us glimpses of the possibilities of the human spirit. Isn't there a kind of sample brotherhood in the making of music: just a sample, under conditions that are transitory, but one which might grow if it could be remembered and nurtured? I thought about it that night on the plane. I had thought about it often before. I had tried several times, even, to

38

get it into writing: the fun, the warmth, the affection, the integrity, the forgetfulness of self, that can be a part of making music. Can *they* be glimpses of brotherhood? They had been, I thought, for me, and I had a feeling that night that they drew me homeward even more powerfully than the plane's engines.

At home, I told myself, was an art higher, perhaps, than the old world has yet understood. "The musical ear," Boston schoolteachers informed their Mayor in 1838, "is more common than has been generally supposed." Boston, that was! Boston, Massachusetts, not Vienna or Munich or London. The musical ear lets people make music. Its commonness—recognized in America—lets them make music together.

Making music together is hard work that is fun. Making music together creates a kind of brotherhood where failure is everybody's loss, where success is a victory for all, where differences of pigmentation and inherited beliefs have no relevance. *We, my dear friends, do it here.* We create a new world for a few moments; we are, for a time, together in pastures green; . . . and remembering, wish the whole world could be like that, forever.

V

Our Primeval Pact

I HOPE it will not be too much of a surprise if I begin by saying that I have a few very dear friends. With them I feel free to discuss such things as religion and wisdom and art and gardening— or we can have a comfortable kind of understanding just by keeping silent.

Some of these friends I seldom see: they live too far away from Pittsburgh. But occasionally, by exchanging letters, I remind myself that the world is yet comfortable because we are both still in it. I sometimes work hard at such letters—almost as hard as I work at letters I know I will never send—and some of the answers have furnished important parts of my education.

One of those letters, from a very great but sometimes terribly misunderstood man, was an answer to my attempt to tell him that some of the seeds he had planted were growing. I tried to tell him a little about this choir: what it does to its members and to its director.

Once or twice a year you ask me to talk to you and at those times I can find no other subject than what being a part of the Heinz Chapel Choir does to us. That seems to me to be important.

My friend gave me an answer in his letter. He ended with "all hail affection" which he knew was part of the answer, but the sentence which dropped things into place for me was this: "You have discovered much of the primeval pact between your world and yourselves." I want to say that again; I want it to stay in your minds for the next few minutes: "*You have discovered much of the primeval pact between your world and yourselves.*"

The discoveries I think my friend was talking about have to be made over and over again. They will be new to many of you as you come upon them, and the looks on your faces will renew them for me.

Last fall another of my friends asked me which choir was the best of all the choirs I have had here since 1938. He took me by surprise; I had never asked myself that question. I had thought of it as all one choir: a kind of chain leading back, each link wrought with exceeding care and affection, the best we could do with that metal and hammer and anvil and fire. But I tried to answer the question, and I said that not separate choirs but quite definite high moments stood out in my memory. I could have listed a great many, but our chatting was using his valuable time, so I told of only two. Both of them involved choir members who represented the whole span of the choir's life: the perform-ance of the Bach Cantata last Palm Sunday—which we can rehear on the recording—and Brother James' Air at the "sing" after Sunday dinner at camp last fall.

Brother James' Air, that beautiful Sunday before we came back to classes, sounded for me with a serenity we had never before achieved. About a third of us were from last year's choir, a third were new members who must have been wondering what exactly this was all about, and about thirty were graduates who were renewing an experience which had been very dear. All of just that group had never sung that song together before. But some of us were discovering, and many of us reaffirming, a part of that primeval pact: "And in my Father's heart alway my dwelling place shall be." It was a new sense of meaning for a beloved sym-bol already packed with meaning.

I, and a few of you, if we think about it, know why that tremendous passage from Paul's first letter to the Corinthians is an inevitable part of our Sunday at camp. I don't remember who first chose it, but it was someone who was making his pact. When all of you understand why it was there, you will have begun yours. It has a connection with Brother James'—and our—serene and shining psalm.

Our pact with our world, our compact with ourselves, is sometimes misunderstood. It surprises and dismays us that some of those whose trust we greatly crave should be unable to comprehend it. About a third of us each year are new, but seldom does any one of *them* make us feel that they have arrived in the middle of a play which makes only bad sense.

Does this really look from the outside like a gray-haired man who should know better exploiting fifty innocent young people for his own profit? Is this a group of conceited singers putting on a show in that lovely Chapel only for praise and acclaim? So I have been told! But that is not a part of our pact with our world, and to be told that it is, is not really convincing but heartbreaking. It is not said in the spirit of that advice to the people at Corinth who, coming late, were so sure that they already had seen the play.

We know from what we do together, and it is a part of our pact, that in our togetherness we can do what none of us could possibly do alone. We come to trust each other, to have confidence that our work together will represent our very best: it is part of our pact with our world. We know that when we do our best we often feel a Presence, a Power, that makes our total best greater than the sum of all our own individual bests. If the exaltation of such moments, which must be visible in our faces, and which remains forever in our memories, is conceit, it is the conceit of Another, not ours. It is part of our pact, our world.

But we are quite ordinary human beings, and perhaps this exaltation is not, for us, a glimpse of the divine, an intimation of the spirit of God. But perhaps it is as close as our poor spirits will come, and it might be that our experience is trying to tell us that *the human spirit and the spirit of God are indivisible.* Even that could be part of our primeval pact with our world!

Perhaps, then, our anxiety to do our very best, our efforts to achieve some moments of perfection, our conceit, our pride, are really a search for a kind of glory which must also be a part of our pact.

Is there such a glory?

This was the modern Stranger in Limbo, talking to the Shade, the ghost of Socrates: "The founder of our spiritual city saw in God, whom he called his Father, a great lover of life, as you, too, once called him: but not a lover of human life only, or of any life only in its perfection. His hand had scattered bountifully throughout the chaos of matter the seeds of all sorts of perfections, setting *the love and the need of a special perfection in each creature's heart;*[1] but the path of any incarnate spirit, buried as it must be in matter and beset by accidents, is necessarily long and perilous; and few there are who ever reach the goal. Yet the perfections of all those who fall by the way and never attain perfection are none the less present for ever to the mind of God, and a part of his glory: and such of us as have no glory here may be content with our glory there."[2]

I suspect, my friends, that human and ordinary and mortal as we are, a little glory *there* will show on our faces, in our voices, and will become a part of our primeval pact with our world.

---

[1] My italics.

[2] George Santayana, *Dialogues in Limbo;* "The Philanthropist."